FRANCESCO GIOIA

Paul
of Tarsus

The apostle for all to know

Libreria Editrice Vaticana

Paolo di Tarso - l'apostolo che tutti devono conoscere

English translation:
A. J. O'Brien

© Copyright 2002
Pontificia Amministrazione
della Patriarcale Basilica di S. Paolo

ISBN 88-209-7293-X

Cover
St. Paul.
Detail from the absidal mosaic,
Basilica of St. Paul outside the Walls - Rome

Back Cover
Arms of St. Paul
Cloister of the Basilica
of St. Paul outside the Walls - Rome

Preface

While Paul is undoubtedly its greatest genius, he is not "the second founder of Christianity", as claimed by Wilhelm Wrede (1859-1906)[1].

An unequivocal sign of the importance of Paul's message is the number of monographs on his life and works published every year throughout the world. This great Apostle, however, remains little known among the people.

While attentive to the demands of scientific research, this present volume is intended as a popular work to assist those who want to have at least an outline of the life and thought of this great Christian writer, but are unable to undertake formal systematic study for various reasons.

The following few pages condense all the biographical details available to us from Paul's letters, and from the Acts of the Apostles, written by Luke, Paul's first biographer.

---

[1] W. Wrede, *Paulus*. Tuebingen 1904, p.104. With some qualifications, the same thesis is supported by two Jewish scholars: J. Klausner and H. J. Schoeps who regard Jesus as a pious Jew and Paul as an apostate.

Numerous passages from Paul's letters are cited in order to facilitate an initial encounter with his thought and to afford a glimpse of the many sided personality of the greatest ever Christian missionary.

Paul's perennial message can be grasped from the apologia he gave in Caeserea before King Agrippa II (27-95), his dissolute sister Bernice[2] and Festus, the Roman governor of Judaea (60-62), when he was forced to defend himself against the Jews who demanded his death[3].

Having heard the Apostle's discourse which was laced with biographical details and intended to demonstrate the centrality of Christ in his life, Festus shouted out: "Paul, you are out of your mind, all that leaning of yours is driving you mad". Paul replied: "Festus, Your Excellency, I am not mad: I am speaking nothing but the sober truth".

Then he asked the king: "King Agrippa, do you believe in the prophets? I know you do". Agrippa replied: "a little more and your arguments would make a Christian of me". It is impossible to say whether these remarks are subtly ironic or intended to convey a veiled scepticism or whether they are to be taken positively.

Paul concluded with a stinging witticism: "I wish before God that not only you but all who have

---

[2] Cf. Acts 25,24.
[3] Both were children of Herod Agrippa I who had beheaded James, the brother of John. "When he saw that this pleased the Jews, he decided to arrest Peter as well" (Acts 12,2-3).

heard me to-day would come to be as I am - except for these chains"[4].

The Apostle's conclusion expresses his profound desire that the hour of salvation would come for all. Writing to Timothy he openly states as much: *"God our saviour ...wants everyone to be saved and reach full knowledge of the truth"*[5].

Paul of Tarsus, whom all should know, says the same thing to us to-day: *"Brothers, all I ask is that you should copy me as I copied you"*[6]. *"Take me for your model, as I take Christ"*[7].

+ Francesco Gioia
Pontifical Administrator
of the Patriarchal Basilica of St. Paul

Rome, 25 January 2002, *Feast of the Conversion of St. Paul, the Apostle.*

---

[4] Acts 26, 24-29.
[5] 1 Tim 2,4; cf. 4,10.
[6] Gal 4,12.
[7] 1Cor 11,1.

1. Biographical Outline

Paul was known by two names, *Paulos*[1] and *Saulos*[2]. He was born in Tarsus[3] between 15 and 5 B.C.[4]. We know that he was a "young" man when he took part in the stoning of Stephen[5] (about the year 36). He is described as "old" when he wrote to Philemon[6] from a Roman prison sometime between 61 and 63 A.D..

Paul describes himself as a Jew of the diaspora: "I was born of the race of Israel and of the tribe of Benjamin[7], a Hebrew born of Hebrew parents, and I was circumcised when I was eight days old. As for the Law, I was a Pharisee; as for working for religion, I was a persecutor of the Church; as

---

[1] Cf. Acts 13,9; Rm 1,1; Gal 1,1.

[2] Cf. Acts 7,58; 8,1.

[3] Tarsus was an important cultural and trading centre at the time. Many Jews, including Paul's parents, had settled there. The Apostle was proud of the fact that he had been born in Tarsus and stated as much to the Roman military authorities: "I am a Jew and a citizen of the well-known city of Tarsus in Cilicia" (Acts 21,39). He returned to his native city having been forced to leave Jerusalem because of a conspiracy against him led by the hellenistic Jews (Acts 9,30). For almost four years, he remained there, until Barnabas came in search of his help in evangelizing Antioch of Syria (Acts 11,25), after which we have no further explicit references to his having returned to Tarsus. It is possible that he may have passed through Tarsus with Silas on his second mission when he crossed Syria and Cilicia (cf. Acts 15,41), and possibly during the following mission when he set out for Galatia and Phrygia from Antioch of Syria (Acts 18,23).

[4] Cf. Acts 21,39

[5] Cf. Acts 7,58.

[6] Cf. Phm 9.

[7] Saul, the first king of Israel, from whom Paul took his name, also belonged to the tribe of Benjamin (cf. 1 Sam 10,20-21).

far as the Law can make you perfect, I was faultless"[8].

He speaks again of his early formation in his defense discourse, given in Hebrew, when he was arrested by the Roman triune following on the Jewish rebellion in the temple in Jerusalem: "I am a Jew...and was born in Tarsus in Cilicia. I was brought up here in this city (Jerusalem). I studied under Gamaliel and was taught the exact observance of the Law of our ancestors. In fact I was as full of duty towards God as you are to-day"[9].

From this we can infer that Paul belonged to a Jewish family of Palestinian origin, that still used Aramaic, as distinct from the "hellenic" Jews. His must have been a well-off family, as can be concluded from the fact that he enjoyed Roman citizenship from birth, and from having been sent to study in Jerusalem.

In accordance with Jewish tradition, the young Saul was taught not only the law but also a manual trade, in this case, "tent-making"[10]. This trade enabled him to earn what was necessary to live on without being a burden to the communities that he founded. Proudly, he tells the elders of Ephesus: "I have never asked anyone for money or clothes; you know for yourselves that the work I did earned enough to meet my needs and those of my companions"[11].

With regard to his physical appearance, we have no objective information, except for a few com-

---

[8] Phil 3,5-6.
[9] Acts 2,3;cf. 26,5; 2 Cor 11,22; Phil 3,6.
[10] Cf. Acts 18,3.
[11] Acts 20,33-34; cf. 1 Cor 4,12; 2 Cor 12,13; 18,3; 1 Thes 2,9; 2 Thes 3,8.

St. Paul
Late XIII century
Sanctum Sanctorum
Sanctuary of the Holy Stairs - Rome

ments in his epistles: "you see only half a man"[12], he suffered from an illness[13], and he had a mysterious "thorn in the flesh"[14]. He must, however, have had physically robust. He survived stoning, harsh flogging, three ship wrecks, during one of which he spent "an entire day and a night on the open sea", he survived numerous travels, thirst, hunger, frequent fasts, cold and exposure[15].

The second century apocryphal *Acts of Paul* has preserved the following description: "He was a man of low stature, bald, with bandy legs, of fine aspect, close eyebrows, his nose largely flattened, graceful, sometimes looking like a man, others times appearing like an angel".

In the *Acts of the Apostles*, Luke describes him as seething with "threats to slaughter the Lord's disciples"[16]. Indeed, he took part in the killing of Stephen[17], as he acknowledges himself: "I even persecuted this Way [of Jesus] to the death and sent women as well as men to prison in chains, as the high priest and the whole council of elders can testify, since they sent me with letters to their brothers in Damascus. When I set off, it was with the intention of bringing prisoners back from there to Jerusalem for punishment"[18].

On the road to Damascus, about 230 kilometres from Jerusalem, he received the revelation of the "Son of God"[19], abjured and experienced his famous conversion.

This is the description given in his apologia before the Jewish people in Jerusalem: "I was on

---

[12] 2 Cor 10,10.
[13] Gal 4,13.
[14] 2 Cor 12,7.
[15] Cf. 2Cor 11,24-26.
[16] Acts 9,1.

[17] Cf. Acts 7,58; 8,1; 22,20.
[18] Acts 22,4-5; cf. 8,3; Gal 1,13-14; Phil 3,6.
[19] Cf. Gal 1,16.

that journey and nearly at Damascus when about midday a bright light from heaven suddenly shone around me. I fell to the ground and I heard a voice saying, 'Saul, Saul' why are you persecuting me?'. I answered: Who are you Lord? and he said to me, 'I am Jesus the Nazarene, and you are persecuting me'. The people with me saw the light but did not hear his voice as he spoke to me. I said: What am I to do Lord? The Lord answered: 'Stand up and go into Damascus, and there you will be told what you have been appointed to do'. The light had been so dazzling that I was blind and my companions had to take me by the hand; and so I came to Damascus. Someone called Ananias, a devout follower of the Law and highly thought of by all the Jews living there, came to see me; he stood beside me and said, 'Brother Saul, receive your sight'. Instantly, my sight came back and I was able to see him. Then he said: 'The God of our ancestors has chosen you to do his will, to see the Just One and hear his own voice speaking, because you are to be his witness before all mankind, testifying to what you have seen and heard. And now, why delay? It is time you were baptized and had your sins washed away while invoking his name'"[20].

For Paul, conversion is a second birth, divesting him of the "old man", transforming him into a "new man"[21] and completely changing his previous thought, will and life. Everything that he had previously valued, he now despises in order to gain Christ[22].

---

[20] Acts 22,6-16; cf. Acts 9,1-19; 26,12-18.
[21] Cf. Col 3,9; Eph 4,24.
[22] Cf. Phil 3,7-8.

Paul could never compromise. As a Jew, he was unreservedly for Moses and the Law. Following his conversion, his only object in life was Christ: "Life to me, of course, is Christ"[23]. That name that he had previously hated and for which he had sent men and women to prison now dominates his mind and heart, having become the source of all his activities. To the Galatians he revealed the source of his limitless dedication: "faith in the Son of God who loved me and sacrificed himself for my sake"[24]. He placed his entire self, everything that he was and possessed at the service of Jesus Christ so that he might be loved by all nations[25]. Once conquered by Jesus Christ, his whole life became a "race" towards him[26].

Although chosen by God from his mother's womb[27], Paul was not always an apostle. Rather, he became one. He saw himself as the "least of the Apostles", "born when no one expected it"[28]. Never the less, he boasts that he is "the chosen apostle"[29].

While Peter is the Apostle to the Jews[30], Paul defines himself as the "apostle to the Gentiles"[31], even though he began his preaching in the synagogues of various cities. It was after the Jews' rejection of the Gospel message that Paul turned exclusively to the pagans, as happened in

---

[23] Phil 1,21.
[24] Gal 2,20.
[25] Cf. Rm 1,14; 15,16.
[26] Cf. Phil 3,12.
[27] Cf. Gal 1,15.
[28] Cf. 1 Cor 15,8-9.
[29] Cf. Rm 1,1; 1 Tim 2,7; 2 Tim 1,11; 2 Cor 5,16.
[30] Cf. Gal 2,7.
[31] Rm 11,13; cf. 15,16. 18; Acts 18,6; 22,21; 26,20; Gal 1,16; 2,2. 8-9; Col 1,27; 1 Thes 2,16; 1 Tim 2,7; 3,16.

Anthioch in Pisidia: "We had to proclaim the Word of God to you first, but since you have rejected it, since you do not think yourselves worthy of eternal life, we must turn to the pagans. For this is what the Lord commanded us to do"[32]. Shortly before his death in Rome, he convoked the "most prominent Jews" to "convince them about Christ". Following on their rejection he says: "Understand, then, that this salvation of God is sent to the pagans; they will listen to it"[33]. This rejection was a source of great sorrow and pain for Paul to the extent that was prepared to be separated from Christ for the sake of his brothers, and [his own] flesh and blood"[34].

Paul did not arbitrarily assume the task of preaching the Gospel. This duty was conferred on him from on high and confirmed by those who were the "pillars of the Church"[35]. He unconditionally devoted himself to his mandate and he allowed no obstacle to stop or impede his apostolic zeal.

Paul mainly carried out his apostolic mission during three journeys undertaken in the years 47-49 and 57-58, covering over 7,800 kilometres on foot and 9,000 at sea, despite a particularly severe chronic illness[36]. Together with a few collaborators, especially Timothy, he founded the communities of Galatia, Ephesus, Colossae in Asia, Thessalonica and Philippi in Macedonia, Corinth in Acaia. With the world as his objective, he set out from Antioch[37], hoping to reach Spain which was then the farthest end of the known world[38].

---

[32] Acts 13,45-47.
[33] Acts 28,29.
[34] Rm 9,2-3.
[35] Cf. Gal 1,11-12; 2,9-10.
[36] Cf. Gal 4,13.
[37] Acts 13,1-3.
[38] Cf. Rm 15,28.

His "days and nights" was spent preaching and working[39] in celebrating the liturgy[40] and catechizing[41] and in the tedious labour of dictating letters[42].

According the earliest traditions, Paul was martyred in the year 67[43] close to Tre Fontane on the outskirts of Rome. The faithful buried his body in the place where the great basilica of St Paul without the walls would later be erected[44]. Shortly before his death, he wrote to Timothy saying: "As for me, my life is already being poured away as a libation, and the time has come for me to be gone. I have fought the good fight to the end; I have run the race to the finish; I have kept the faith; all that is to come now is the crown of righteousness reserved for me, which the Lord, the righteous judge, will give to me on that Day; and not only to me but to all those who have longed for his Appearing"[45].

---

[39] Cf. 1 Thes 2,9.

[40] Cf. Acts 20,7.

[41] Cf.Acts 16,31-34; 18,8; 20,20; 28,16-24.

[42] Cf. Rm 16,22; 1 Cor 5,9; 2 Cor 7,8; 10,9-10; Col 4, 16; 1 Thes 5,27; 2 Thes 2,2.15; 3,14.

[43] Saint Jerome suggests the year 67 (*De viris illustribus*, 5 and 12); The *Chronica* of Eusebius mentions the year 68, while other scholars advance different hypotheses.

[44] The oldest references to the tomb of the Apostle Paul come from the priest Gaius at the end of the second century: "I can show you the monuments of the Apostles. If you go to the Vatican or to the Ostien way, you will find the monuments of the founders of this Church" (Eusebius of Caeseria, *Historia Ecclesiastica*, 2,22,2). A later tradition, not earlier than the fourth or fifth century, mentions that Paul was martyred by decapitation at the Aquae Silviae, known to-day as Tre Fontane (*Acta Petri et Pauli*, 80).

[45] 2 Tim 4, 6-8.

Conversion of St. Paul
Codex reg. Lat 90
Apostolic Library
Vatican City

Martyrdom of St. Paul
Miniature from the Carmina of Prudentius
Codex urb. Lat. 666, fol, 6v.
Apostolic Library
Vatican City

2. The Letters

When he was unable to travel during the winter, Paul spent his time writing letters in Greek to the communities he had founded (the epistle to the Romans and to his friends Philemon, Timothy and Titus are exceptions to this general rule).

Tradition holds that he wrote 14 letters. To-day, however, it is accepted that Paul is not the author of the epistle to the Hebrews. Of the remaining thirteen, seven are regarded as authentic and their pauline authorship is beyond any doubt: 1 Thessalonians; 1-2 Corinthians; Galatians; Romans; Philippians; and Philemon.

The epistles to the Philippians, Philemon, Colossians and Ephesians are known as his letters from prison because they have been traditionally regarded as having been written during two periods of detention: the epistle to the Philippians written in 57 from his prison in Ephesus, while the others belong to the period between 62-63 and were written from his prison in Rome. The epistles to Timothy and Titus are known as the "pastoral epistles" since they were addressed to pastors.

Some scholars have raised doubts with regard to the pauline authorship of 2 Thessalonians, Colossians, Ephesians, 1 and 2 Timothy, and Titus. They hold that these epistles were written by Paul's disciples who had assimilated his thought. They ascribed the letters to him so as to invest them with greater authority. This is known as pseudographology which is well known in both the biblical and classical traditions. For example, the Pentateuch, or first five books of the Bible, are attributed to Moses while the Iliad and the Odyssey are attributed to Homer.

Aside from this doubt concerning the Pauline authorship of these epistles, it has to be understood that all 14 letters traditionally attributed to the Apostle are none the less important for the Church because they are the oldest writings in the New Testament and ante-date the Gospels. Paul wrote the epistle to the Thessalonians from Corinth around the year 50 or 51, while the first Gospel, now generally regarded as that of Mark, was written between 65 and 70. Paul was therefore the first to write about Christ.

The predominant and essential point of the letters is the person of Christ whose "slave"[46] Paul declares himself to be. He was so profoundly immersed in Christ that he writes: "I live now not with my own life but with the life of Christ who lives in me"[47]. Christ is the profound "I" of Paul.

The Church is regarded as the "mystical body"[48]. With regard to the Mother of Christ, Paul makes only indirect reference: "born of a woman"[49].

His style, however, lacks the elegance of the classical writers of antiquity. Paul admits as much himself: "I am not a polished speechmaker, but as for knowledge that is a different matter"[50]. The second letter to the Corinthians says: "He writes powerful and strong-worded letters"[51].

Not infrequently they contain anacolutha, parentheses, elision, and irregular syntax. Some-

---

[46] Cf. Rm 1,1; Gal 1,10; Phil 1,1; Tit 1,1.
[47] Gal 2,20.
[48] Cf. 1 Cor 12,12-27; Rm 12,4-5; Col 1,18; Eph 1,22-23; 5,23.30.
[49] Gal 4,4.
[50] 2 Cor 11,6.
[51] Cf. 2 Cor 10,10.

times his sentences are heavy. Paul could well agree with Epictetus: "As for composing elegant phrases, I leave that to others"[52].

His style is permeated with recurring antitheses: Adam-Christ[53], flesh-Spirit[54], letter-Spirit[55], faith-works[56], wisdom-foolishness[57], weakness-power[58], slavery-liberty[59], old man-new man[60]. His thought is often transmitted by eloquent metaphors drawn from sport[61], nature[62], building[63], the human body[64], maternity or paternity[65], and worship[66].

---

[52] Epictetus, *Lectures*, II, I, 33; cf. III, 9, 14; 23,27.
[53] Cf. Rm 5,14-21.
[54] Cf. Gal 5, 16-25.
[55] Cf. 2 Cor 3,6.
[56] Cf. Rm 3,4.
[57] Cf. 1 Cor 1,18-25.
[58] Cf. 2 Cor 12,7-10.
[59] Cf. Gal 5,1-13.
[60] Cf. Rm 6,6; 2 Cor 5,17.
[61] Cf. 1 Thes 2,1-2; 4,8; 1 Cor 9, 24-27, Gal 2,2; 5,7; Phil 2,16; 2 Tim 4,6-8.
[62] Cf. 1 Cor 3,4-8; 14, 35-44.
[63] Cf. 1 Cor 3,9; 1 Thes 5,11; Eph 2,19-22; 4,12.
[64] Cf. 1 Cor 11,3-16; 12,12-27; 15,35-58; Rm 12,4-5; Eph 4,15-16.
[65] Cf. 1 Thes 2,3-12; Gal 4,16-20; Phm 10.
[66] Cf. 1 Cor 3,16-17; 2 Cor 6,16; Eph 2,21.

St. Paul
Fresco by the circle of Antoniazzo Romano
Basilica of St. Paul outside the Walls - Rome

3. Paul's Successes and Failures as recounted in the Acts of the Apostles

Luke dedicates the greater narrative part of the *Acts of the Apostles* to Paul. He preserves for us several incidents from his life, his conversion, his imprisonment in Rome and even some of his discourses.

A close reading of Luke's account of the apostolic journeys of Paul reveals one thing: in every city where Paul proclaimed Christ, his successes were always accompanied by failures.

In Damascus, having just converted to Christ, he began "preaching fearlessly in the name of the Lord"[67]; "he was able to throw the Jewish colony in Damascus into complete confusion by the way he demonstrated that Jesus was the Christ"; but they became so irritated with him that they "worked out a plot to kill him"[68].

In Jerusalem "Saul started to go around with them...preaching fearlessly the name of the Lord. But after he had spoken to the Hellenists, and argued with them, they became determined to kill him"[69].

In Cyprus, he encountered the false Jewish prophet, Bar-jesus, called Elimas, who tried to lure the Proconsul, Sergius Paulus, away from the faith[70].

In the synagogue at Antioch in Pisidia, Paul and Barnabas were invited to address "the people with some words of encouragement". Paul demonstrated how "it was to our ancestors that

---

[67] Acts 9,27.
[68] Acts 9, 22-23.
[69] Acts 9,28-29.
[70] Cf. Acts 13,8.

God made the promise, but it is to us, their children, that he has fulfilled it by raising Jesus from the dead". This preaching caused "many Jews and devout converts to follow Paul and Barnabas"[71]. On the following Sabbath, both missionaries were again invited to preach. This time, however, the results were different: "When they saw the crowds, the Jews, prompted by jealousy, used blasphemies and contradicted everything Paul said. Then Paul and Barnabas spoke out boldly: 'We had to proclaim the word of God to you first, but since you have rejected it, since you do not think yourselves worthy of eternal life, we must turn to the pagans...' But the Jews worked upon some of the devout women of the upper classes and the leading men of the city and persuaded them to turn against Paul and Barnabas and expel them from the territory"[72].

The preaching of Paul and Barnabas also had a dual effect among the congregation of Iconia: "A great many Jews and Greeks became believers. Some of the Jews, however, refused to believe and they poisoned the minds of the pagans against the brothers. Accordingly, Paul and Barnabas stayed on for some time, preaching fearlessly for the Lord. In the end, however, their adversaries prevailed: "a move was made by pagans as well as Jews to make attacks on them and to stone them. When the apostles came to hear of this, they went off to Lyconia for safety"[73].

In Lystra, following on Paul's curing of the cripple, "some Jews arrived from Antioch and Iconium, and turned the people against the apostles.

---

[71] Acts 13,15.32-33.43.
[72] Acts 13,44.50.
[73] Acts 14,1-6.

They stoned Paul and dragged him outside the town, thinking he was dead"[74].

At Philippi, Lydia, a merchant in the purple-dye trade, converted and invited Paul and Silas to stay at her house. Paul drove out a demon from a slave who "made a lot of money for her masters by telling fortunes". When the masters saw there was no hope of making further money out of her, they seized Paul and Silas and dragged them to the law courts in the market place and charged them with proselytism. For this they were beaten and thrown into prison. Subsequently, the magistrates who had condemned them had to ask for pardon since they should not have been flogged because they were Roman citizens[75].

Following on the failures and prison in Philippi, Paul and Silas arrived in Thessalonica. Their preaching was successful: "Some of them were convinced and joined Paul and Silas, and so did a great many God-fearing people and Greeks, as well as a number of rich women". This created a reaction among the Jews who, "full of resentment, enlisted the help of a gang from the market place, stirred up a crowd, and so had the whole city in uproar". They dragged both missionaries before the magistrates and accused them of having broken every one "of Caesar's edicts" by "claiming that there was another emperor, Jesus". Having paid sureties they were released[76]. In his first epistle to the Thessalonians, Paul recounts that "We had, as you know, been given rough treatment and been grossly insulted at Philippi, and it was our God who gave us the

---

[74] Acts 14,19.
[75] Acts 16, 14-39.
[76] Acts 17,4-9;
cf. 1 Thes 2,14.

courage to proclaim his Good News in the face of great opposition"[77].

In Beroea, the word of God was accepted "very readily", but the Jews of Thessalonica came and "to make trouble and stir up the people", forcing Paul to leave for Athens[78].

The reaction of the Athenians to Paul's famous discourse on the Areopagus was mixed: some thought him a charlatan, and a "propagandist for some outlandish gods", while others "derided" him saying: "We would like to hear you talk about this again". But "there were some who attached themselves to him and became believers"[79].

When the Jews of Corinth heard Paul declare that Jesus was the Christ, "they turned against him and began to insult him; they made a concerted attack on Paul and brought him before the tribunal"[80]. The Lord consoled Paul in a dream: "Do not be afraid to speak out, nor allow yourself to be silenced: I am with you. I have so many people on my side in this city that no one will attempt to hurt you"[81].

At Ephesus, "He began by going to the Synagogue, where he spoke out boldly and argued persuasively about the kingdom of God. He did this for three months, till the attitude of some of the congregation hardened into unbelief. As soon as they began attacking the Way in front of the others, he broke with them and took his disciples apart to hold daily discussions in the lecture room of Tyrannus. This went on for two years, with the result that people from all over Asia, both Jews

---

[77] 1 Thes 2,2.
[78] Cf. Acts 17,11-15.
[79] Cf. Acts 17,18.32-34.
[80] Acts 18, 5-6.12.
[81] Acts 18,9-10.

The Apostle Paul
Mosaic
Sts. Cosmas and Damien - Rome

and Greeks, were able to hear the word of the Lord"[82].

Although Paul's presence in Ephesus was accompanied by miracles[83], the silversmiths feared that his preaching would compromise the sale of "silver shrines of Diana". They conspired against him and forced the Apostle to leave for Macedonia[84]. In the presence of the elders of the Church of Ephesus, who had come to meet him in Miletus, Paul confessed: "I have served the Lord in all humility, with all the sorrows and trials that came to me through the plots of the Jews"[85].

On his way to Jerusalem, his ship put in at Tyre and the disciples there counselled him not to go to Jerusalem for "he would be bound by the Jews and delivered into the hands of the pagans". Paul's response clearly demonstrates his courage: "What are you trying to do-weaken my resolution by your tears? For my part, I am ready not only to be tied up but even to die in Jerusalem for the name of the Lord Jesus Christ"[86].

As foreseen, the people in Jerusalem, incited by the Jews in Asia, "tried to kill him". Only the Tribune's intervention saved him. He "arrested Paul and had him bound in two chains"[87]. Paul's account of his vocation and his explanation of his apostolate enraged the Jews of Jerusalem who

---

[82] Acts 19,8-10. Prior to Paul's arrival in the synagogue of Ephesus, "An Alexandrine Jew named Apollos...an eloquent man, with sound knowledge of the scriptures... had preached with great spiritual earnestness" (Acts 18,26).
[83] Cf. Acts 19,11-12.
[84] Cf. Acts 19,23-20,1.
[85] Acts 20,19.
[86] Acts 21,4.11-13.
[87] Acts 21,31.33.

called on the Tribune: "Take him from us, he does not deserve to live". His Roman citizenship saved him from being flogged, but he was forced to appear before the Sanhedrin. Ananias, the High Priest, ordered his servants to strike him on the mouth, but he courageously defended his religious choice: "Brothers, to this day, I have conducted myself before God with a perfectly clear conscience". His reference to the resurrection caused a heated controversy to break out among the Pharisees and the Sadducees. Thus, the Tribune, fearing that Paul would be ambushed, had him escorted to the fortress of Jerusalem. The Jews, however, did not give up. About forty of them "lay in wait for him, and they vowed not to eat or drink until they [had] got rid of him"[88].

In these circumstances, the word did not fail to comfort Paul, despite his tribulations: "Courage! You have borne witness to me in Jerusalem, now you must do the same in Rome"[89].

To avoid Paul's falling into the hands of those who had conspired against him, the Tribune had him escorted to Caesarea, where he remained a prisoner for two years, although his case had been placed before the governor, Felix[90].

Being a Roman citizen[91], Paul appealed to Caesar[92]. As "it seemed pointless to send a prisoner [to Rome] without indicating the charges against him[93], he was brought before King Agrippa, where he defended himself "with assurance"[94].

---

88 Cf. Acts cc. 22-23,21.
89 Acts 23,11.
90 Cf. Acts cc. 23,23-24,27.
91 Cf. Acts 16,37; 22,25-27.
92 Cf. Acts 25,11-12.
93 Acts 25,27.
94 Acts 26,26.

Having survived several journeys, including a shipwreck[95], Paul reached Rome where the brethren in the faith went out to welcome him. He "gave thanks to God and took heart"[96]. Here too, as in the past[97], he first preached his message to the Jews. "Some were convinced by what he said, while the rest were sceptical"[98].

Division among the Jews is a recurring theme in Paul's preaching[99]. The time, however, had come to close the question. The Apostle, referring to Isaiah who had foreseen the blindness of his own people[100], once again solemnly proclaimed the definitive exclusion of the Jews and the election of the Gentiles[101], as he had done in Antioch in Pisidia[102].

In Rome, Paul spent two whole years under guard in a rented house "proclaiming the Kingdom of God and teaching the truth about the Lord Jesus Christ, with complete freedom and without hindrance"[103].

Luke thus concludes his account of the spread of the Gospel from Jerusalem "to the ends of the earth"[104], demonstrating that the vision with which he opens the *Acts of the Apostles* had been realized, and he proposes Paul as the supreme model of the courageous and untiring missionary.

---

[95] Cf. Acts 27,9-43.
[96] Acts 28,15.
[97] Acts 13,5.
[98] Acts 28,17.24.
[99] Cf. Acts 14,1-2; 17,2-5; 18,5-6; 19,8-9; 23,9-10.
[100] Cf. Is 6,9-10.
[101] Cf. Acts 28,28.
[102] Cf. Acts 13,46-17.
[103] Acts 28,16.30-31.
[104] Acts 1,8.

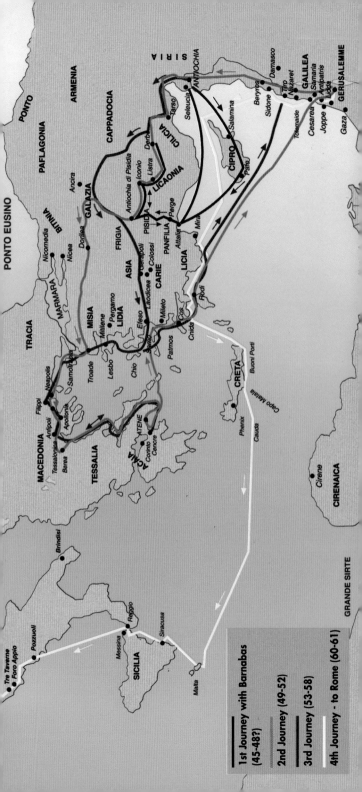

PONTO EUSINO

TRACIA

MACEDONIA
Filippi
Neapoli
Anfipoli
Apollonia
Tessalonica
Berea

TESSALIA

ACAIA
ATENE
Corinto
Cencre

MISIA
Millene
Pergamo
Troade
Lesbo
Chio
Samo
Mileto
Patmos
Cnida
Coo
Rodi

LIDIA
Efeso
Laodicea
Colossi
Ierapoli

ASIA
Doriea

FRIGIA

CARIE

LICIA
Attalia
Mira

PANFILIA
Perge

PISIDIA
Antiochia di Pisidia
Iconio
Listra
Derbe

GALAZIA
Ancira

CAPPADOCIA

BITINIA
Nicomedia
Nicea

MARMARA

PAFLAGONIA

PONTO

ARMENIA

CILICIA
Tarso
Seleucia

LICAONIA

SIRIA
ANTIOCHIA
Beritos
Sidone
Tiro
Damasco

CIPRO
Salamina
Pafo

CRETA
Buoni Porti
Phenix
Capo Malea
Cauda

Patmos

GALILEA
Nazaret
Samaria
Antipatris
Lidda

GERUSALEMME
Cesarea
Tolemaide
Joppe
Gaza

BRINDISI
Brindisi

SICILIA
Reggio
Messina
Siracusa

Pozzuoli
Foro Appio
Tre Taverne

Malta

CIRENAICA
Cirene

GRANDE SIRTE

1st Journey with Barnabas
(45-48?)

2nd Journey (49-52)

3rd Journey (53-58)

4th Journey - to Rome (60-61)

St. Paul
Fresco by Antonio da Viterbo
Basilica of St. Paul outside the Walls - Rome

4. Paul's Personality as gleaned from the Letters

Of the New Testament authors, Paul is the only one who has left us some biographical information in which he presents himself as a model to be followed or in defense of his apostolate[105]. His versatile personality emerges clearly from his letters as well as his temperament, his spiritual fatherhood, his ardor, his vehemence, and the courage with which he proclaimed the Gospel. He gives the distinct image of an inflexible, tireless man, incorrigible before anyone or anything.

Recalling the words of Jesus, he gives a retrospective account of his sufferings: "If they persecuted me, they will persecute you too[106]". Here he means that "anyone who tries to live in devotion to Christ is certain to be attacked"[107], and must "experience many hardships before [entering] the kingdom of God"[108].

His convictions are based on personal experience. In his first epistle to the Corithians he writes: "To this day we go without food and drink and clothes; we are beaten and have no homes; we work for our living with our own hands". His reaction is clearly evangelical: When we are cursed we answer with a blessing; when we are hounded, we put up with it, we are insulted and we answer politely. We are treated as the offal of the world, still to this day, the scum of the earth"[109].

---

[105] Cf. 1 Cor 15,1-11; Gal 1,13-2,21; Phil 1,12-26; 3,2-21; Col 1,24-27; I Tim 1,12-17; 2 Tim 4,6-8.
[106] John 15,20; cf. Mt 10,17-24;Lk 21,12.
[107] 2 Tim 3,12.
[108] Acts 14,22.
[109] 1 Cor 4,11-13.

In his second letter to the Corinthians, written "in deep distress and anguish of mind, and in tears"[110], Paul "boasts" that he is stronger than his adversaries because of his sufferings and because of his "weakness": "Hebrews are they? So am I. Israelites? So am I. Descendants of Abraham? So am I. The servants of Christ? I must be mad to say this, but so am I, and more than they; more because I have worked harder, I have been sent to prison more often, and whipped so many times more, often almost to death. Five times I had the thirty nine lashes from the Jews; three times I have been beaten with sticks; once I was stoned, three times I have been shipwrecked and once adrift on the open sea for a night and a day. Constantly travelling, I have been in danger from rivers, and in danger from brigands, in danger from my own people and in danger from pagans; in danger in the towns, in danger in the open country, danger at sea and danger from the so-called brothers. I have worked and laboured, often without sleep, I have been hungry and thirsty and often starving; I have been in the cold without clothes. And to leave out much more, there is my daily preoccupation: my anxiety for all the churches. When any man has had scruples, I have had scruples with him. When any man is made to fall, I am tortured. If I am to boast, then let me boast in my own feebleness. The God and Father of the Lord Jesus Christ-bless him for ever-knows that I am not lying. When I was in Damascus, the ethnarch of King Aretas put guards around the city to catch me, and I had to be let down over the wall in a hamper, through a win-

---

[110] 2 Cor 2,4.

dow, in order to escape. Must I go on boasting, though there is nothing to be gained by it? But I will move on to the visions and revelations I have had from the Lord. I know a man in Christ who, fourteen years ago, was caught up- whether still in the body or out of the body, I do not know; God knows- right into the third heaven. I do know, however, that this same person-whether in the body or out of the body I do not know God knows- was caught up into paradise and heard things which must not and cannot be put into human language. I will boast about a man like that, but not about anything of my own except my weaknesses. If I should decide to boast, I should not be made to look foolish, because I should only be speaking the truth; But I am not going to, in case anyone should begin to think I am better than he can actually see and hear me to be. In view of the extraordinary nature of these revelations, to stop me from getting too proud I was given a thorn in the flesh, an angel of Satan to beat me and stop me from getting too proud. About this thing, I have pleaded with the Lord three times for it to leave me, but he has said, 'My grace is grace is enough for you; my power is at its best in weakness'. So, I shall be very happy to make my weakness my special boast so that the power of Christ may stay over me, and that is why I am quite content with my weaknesses, and with insults, hardships, persecutions, and the agonies I go through for Christ's sake. For it is when I am weak that I am strong"[111].

Again, he tell the Corinthians: "Even after we had come to Macedonia, however, there was no

---

[111] 2 Cor 11, 21-12,10.

rest for this body of ours. Far from it; we found trouble on all sides; quarrels outside, misgivings inside"[112]. His peace of mind and his perseverance in the mission were constantly tested by severe trials, but he always knew where to find renewed strength: "[we rely not] on ourselves but only on God, who raises the dead to life"[113]. He was fully confident that Christ would be glorified in his body, both in life and in death[114].

Writing to the Romans he declared: "Nothing therefore can come between us and the love of Christ, even if we are troubled or worried, or being persecuted, or lacking food or clothes, or being threatened or even attacked". He knew from personal experience that "these were the trials through which we triumph, by the power of him who loved us". He was absolutely convinced that nothing could separate him from the love of God[115].

In order not to be overcome by their sufferings, the Christians of Ephesus had to be convinced that Jesus gave them the courage "to approach God in complete confidence, through faith in him". Thus he exhorted them: "Never lose confidence just because of the trials that I go thorough on your account: they are your glory"[116].

He had a "thorn"[117] in his body, an incurable illness[118] the nature of which is unknown to us. His soul was troubled by the Churches he had founded[119]. His greatest pain, however, came from the lack of understanding shown to him by the Chris-

---

[112] 2 Cor 7,5.
[113] 2 Cor 1,8-9.
[114] Cf. Phil 1,20.
[115] Rm 8,35-39.
[116] Eph 3,12-13.
[117] Cf. 2 Cor 12,7.
[118] Cf. Gal 4,13-14.
[119] Cf. 2 Cor 11,29.

Martyrdom of the Apostle Paul
Codex urb. Lat. 112f, 419v.
Apostolic Library
Vatican City

tian authorities in Jerusalem[120] and from the Jewish converts to Christ. These latter still clung to Moses, and continued to accommodate the law, the temple, circumcision and other religious practices, as is clear form the decree issued by the so-called Council of Jerusalem[121]. Under the cloak of James' authority[122], some followed Paul around, contradicting his preaching in one place as soon as he left for another, thereby undertaking a kind of counter-mission which went as far as questioning the very legitimacy of his apostolic mandate[123].

Paul went from one town to another proclaiming Christ. With indomitable courage, he bore suffering and misunderstanding: "We are in difficulties on all sides, but never concerned; we see no answer to our problems, but never despair; we have been persecuted, but never deserted; knocked down but never killed; always, wherever we may be, we carry with us in our body the death of Jesus"[124]. Although bearing the same marks as those of Christ's humanity[125], in all his troubles, he was "filled with consolation and [his] joy was overflowing"[126], and certain that his sufferings "make up all that is still to be undergone by Christ[127]". He goes so far as to say: "I am quite content with my weaknesses, and with insults, hardships, persecutions, and the agonies I go through for Christ's sake"[128].

Paul is the instrument chosen by Christ[129] to carry on his work in time. He considered the proclamation of Christ as a specific obligation:

---

[120] Cf. Acts 21,17-21.
[121] Cf. Acts 1,23-25.
[122] Cf. Gal 2,12.
[123] Cf. 2 Cor 11,5-12; 12, 11.
[124] 2 Cor 4,8-10.
[125] Cf. Gal 6,17.
[126] 2 Cor 7,4.
[127] Col 1,24.
[128] 2 Cor 12,10.
[129] Cf. Acts 9,15.

"Not that I do boast of preaching the Gospel, since it is a duty that has been laid on me, I should be punished if I did not preach it"[130]. His life's objective is to preach the Gospel. It matters nothing to him that some proclaim the Gospel for their own personal gain, even when his imprisonment favours them, or that others proclaim it from love "whether from dishonest motives or in sincerity, Christ is proclaimed, and that makes me happy, and I shall continue being happy"[131].

He is fully conscious that the courage needed to proclaim Christ is God's exclusive gift[132] and, as such, he prays God for it: "Never get tired of staying awake to pray for all the saints; and pray for me to be given an opportunity to open my mouth and speak without fear and give out the mystery of the Gospel of which I am an ambassador in chains; pray that in proclaiming it I may speak as boldly as I ought to"[133].

His dedication to the Gospel gradually absorbs his entire life and his whole strength: "I made myself all things to all men in order to save some at any cost; and I still do this for the sake of the Gospel"[134].

Thus he announces the principle supporting him in his apostolate: "Since we have by an act of mercy been entrusted with this work of administration, there is no weakening on our part. On the contrary, we shall have none of the reticence of those who are ashamed, no deceitfulness or watering down of the word of God; but the way we commend ourselves to every human being

---

[130] 1 Cor 9,16.
[131] Phil 1,18.
[132] Cf. 2 Cor 3,4-5.
[133] Eph 6,19-20.
[134] 1 Cor 9,22-23.

with a conscience is by stating the truth openly in the sight of God"[135].

To the Thessalonians he stated the reasons for his preaching: "We had, as you know, been given rough treatment and been grossly insulted at Philippi, and it was our God who gave us the courage to proclaim his Good News to you in the face of great opposition. We have not taken to preaching because we are deluded, or immoral, or trying to deceive anyone; it was God who decided that we were fit to be entrusted with the Good News, and when we are speaking, we are not trying to please men but God, who can read our innermost thoughts. You know very well, and we can swear it before God, that never at any time have our speeches been simply flattery, or a cover for trying to get money; nor have we looked for any special honour from men, either from you or anybody else, when we could have imposed ourselves on you with full weight, as apostles of Christ"[136].

Nothing was capable of obstructing his path. Race, nations or individuals could not intimidate him. In the same uninhibited way, he addressed himself to his fellow Jews, Greeks, Romans, to the educated and uneducated. He engaged those on the docks of Corinth as well as the sophists of the Areopagus[137], the governor Festus and King Agrippa[138], and even the soldiers who held him captive[139]. When they struck him, insulted him, persecuted him or threw him into prison, from which he was sometimes freed[140], he did not stop.

---

[135] 2 Cor 4,1-2.
[136] 1 Tes 2,2-6.
[137] Cf. Acts 17,18-21.
[138] Cf. Acts 26,2-29.
[139] Cf. Acts 16,27-34; 28,16.
[140] Cf. Acts 16, 23-27.

Masaccio
St. Paul
National Museum - Pisa

On the subject of abstaining from the foods prohibited by the Law, which had been superseded by the Gospel[141], before Peter he was courageous enough "to oppose him to his face[142]" and even to accuse him of "hypocrisy"[143]. He did not forgive Barnabas, who had defended him before the Apostles[144], and subsequently sought him out in Tarsus and introduced him to the community in Antioch[145]. Indeed, during the second missionary voyage, so great was their disagreement that they had to separate and were never again together[146].

Recalling the teaching of Jesus: "You received without charge, give without charge"[147], Paul preached Gospel without recompense: "in my preaching, to be able to offer the Good News free, and not insist on the rights which the Gospel gives me"[148]. He supported himself by his own labours so as to ensure that he was never a burden to those who had received the Gospel from him[149].

Not only was Paul's mission without personal gain to himself, he was also modest, simple and without any form of pride or boasting. He considered himself the "weakest of all the saints"[150]. His exceptional abilities notwithstanding, Paul told the elders of Ephesus: "I have served the Lord in all humility"[151]. In the first letter to the

---

[141] Cf. Gal 2,7-8.
[142] Gal 2,11.
[143] Cf. Acts 2,13.
[144] Cf. Acts 9,26-27.
[145] Cf. Acts 11,25.
[146] Cf. Acts 15,39.
[147] Mt 10,8.
[148] Cf. 1 Cor 9,18; 2 Cor 11,7.
[149] Cf. Acts 20,33-34; cf. 1 Cor 4,12; 2 Cor 12,13; 18,3; 1 Thes 2,9; 2 Thes 3,8.
[150] Eph 3,8.
[151] Acts 20,19.

Corinthians, he writes: "When I came to you, it was not with any show of oratory or philosophy, but simply to tell you what God had guaranteed. During my stay with you, the only knowledge I claimed to have was about Jesus, and only about him as the crucified Christ. Far from relying on any power of my own, I came among you in great 'fear and trembling'"[152].

Paul's humility, however, did not preclude offering himself several times as a model for his faithful: "I beg you to copy me"[153]. Sometimes his style is imperious and his language sharp[154], especially when he curbing the arrogance and pride of the faithful, or those troubling the nascent and struggling communities. It is also true that he arrived in Corinth humble and submissive: "I came among you in fear and trembling"[155], explaining that he did not wish to substitute himself for Christ: "For it is not ourselves that we are preaching, but Christ Jesus as the Lord". He had become their "slave" simply and solely "for Jesus' sake"[156]. He was merely a mediator of Christ, as

---

[152] 1 Cor 2,1-3.

[153] Cf. 1 Cor 4,16; 11,1; Phil 3,17; 2 Thes 3,6; Phil 4,9; 2 Tim 3,10.

[154] His address to those disturbing the community in Galatia is a good example. With sarcasm, he invites them not only to have themselves circumcised but also to emasculation:"Tell those who are disturbing you I would like to see the knife slip" (Gal 5,12). He exhorts the stubborn Galatians (Gal 3,1) to practice charity. If that does not work, he suggests ironically: "If you go snapping at each other and tearing each other to pieces, you had better watch out, or you will destroy the whole community" (Gal 5,15). In warning the Philippians against those preaching circumcision, he says: "Beware of dogs. Watch out for the people who are making mischief. Watch out for the cutters" (Phil 3,2).

[155] 1 Cor 2,3.

[156] 2 Cor 4,5.

such he was dispensable, while Christ "must always reign" in all, and everywhere[157].

The Christians of Corinth were neither exemplary nor the most trustworthy. They were still "sensual men, still infants in Christ"[158]. Despite their rather low social extraction ("how many of you were wise in the ordinary sense of the word, how many were influential people, or came from noble families"[159]), they were proud and arrogant. They aspired to learned discussions to such an extent that Paul was forced to give them a sublime reminder on the manner in which God works, which is very different from that of man: "It was to shame the wise that God chose what is foolish by human reckoning, and to shame what is strong that he chose what is weak by human reckoning; those whom the world thinks nothing at all to show up those who are everything. The human race has nothing to boast about to God"[160]. Precisely because of their pretensions, divisions had broken out among them[161]. They tolerated incest[162]. They placed their disputes before the judges of pagan courts for their decisions[163]. Grave abuses were permitted in the celebration of the Eucharist[164].

Initially, Paul tried a polite approach to this situation but was quite unsuccessful. If anything, it

---

[157] 1 Cor 15,25.

[158] 1 Cor 3,1.

[159] 1 Cor 1,26.

[160] 1 Cor 27-29. In other letters, Paul repeats that God reserves to himself the plan of salvation and its actualization (cf. Rm 3,27; 2 Cor 4,7; Eph 2,9).

[161] Cf. 1 Cor 1,10-13; 2 Cor 12,20.

[162] Cf. 1 Cor 5,2.

[163] Cf. 1 Cor 6,1-7.

[164] Cf. 1 Cor 10,14-30.

further emboldened the trouble makers who accused him of weakness. Then he changed tactics and told them that when he would be present among them, he would demonstrate "with the facts" the same firmness exhibited in his letters[165] and that he was ready "to punish any form of disobedience"[166], even threatening to use the stick with them[167].

Paul was outraged with the trouble makers who disrupted community life, as can be seen from expressions such as "false brethren", "spies"[168], "false apostles", "workers of deceit disguised as apostles of Christ", "ministers of satan" got up as "ministers of justice"[169]. With surprising firmness, in his letter to the Galatians, he writes: "If anyone preaches a version of the Good News different from the one you have already heard, he is to be condemned"[170].

The Apostle always forgave those who offended him[171] with great paternal solicitude: "We were unassuming. Like a mother feeding and looking after her own children, we felt so devoted and protective towards you, and come to love you so much, that we were eager to hand over to you not only the Good News, but our whole lives as well... You can remember how we treated every one of you as a father treats his children, teaching you what was right, encouraging you and appealing to you to live a life worthy of God, who is calling you to share the glory of his kingdom"[172]. To the Galatians he wrote: "My children, I must go through

---

[165] Cf. 2 Cor 10,10.
[166] 2 Cor 10,6.
[167] Cf. 1 Cor 4,21.
[168] Gal 2,4.

[169] 2 Cor 11,13.15.
[170] Gal 1,9.
[171] Cf. 2 Cor 2,10.
[172] 1 Thes 2,7-8.11.

the pain of giving birth to you all over again, until Christ is formed in you"[173]. To the Corinthians, whom he had nourished[174], he says: "I am writing all this not just to make you ashamed but to bring you, as my dearest children, to your senses. You might have thousands of guardians in Christ, but no more than one father and it was I who begot you in Christ Jesus by preaching the Good News"[175].

His own apologia, which is close to "madness"[176], does not derive from pride but from a "concern" that comes from God[177]. A father is always concerned for his children. Likewise, he will not tolerate the disturbance of their faith, especially because they are still insecure, immature and unable to evaluate what they hear about it.

When his correspondents are to be praised, Paul does so generously and redolently[178]. Thus, to the Corinthians, he writes: "I have the very greatest confidence in you, and I am so proud of you"[179]. He does not hesitate, however, if something had to be corrected: "When I wrote to you, in deep distress and anguish of mind, and in tears, it was not to make you feel hurt but to let you know how much love I have for you"[180]. Neither was he sorry for having given correction to them: "Even if I distressed you by my letter, I do

---

[173] Gal 4,19.

[174] Cf. 1 Cor 3,2.

[175] 1 Cor 4,14-15; cf. Phil 10.

[176] Cf. 2 Cor 11,1.16.

[177] Cf. 2 Cor 11,2.

[178] Cf. 1 Cor 8,3-6; 11,2; Gal 4,15; Phil 1,5; 4,14-16; 1 Thes 1,8; 2 Thes 1,4-5.

[179] 2 Cor 7,4.

[180] 2 Cor 2,4.

not regret it. I did regret it before, and I see that that letter did distress you, at least for a time; but I am happy now -not because I made you suffer, but because your suffering led to your repentance"[181]. The hope of leading his children to conversion made him "quite confident"[182] with them.

Courage caused him to reject half measures and opportunism. Paul could well have abandoned the Christians of Corinth or Galatia to their own delusions but that would have been a betrayal and cowardly as far as his mission was concerned. His own conscience knew no compromise: "There is one thing that we are proud of, and our conscience tells us it is true: that we have always treated everybody, and especially you (Corinthians) with the reverence and sincerity which come from God and by the grace of God we have done this without ulterior motives"[183].

Paul is the convinced follower of Christ. He is the courageous and indomitable apostle of Christ who set out to carry the Gospel to whole world. Nothing could stop his zeal or his missionary activities. No one has ever been his equal.

---

[181] 2 Cor 7,8-9.
[182] 2 Cor 3,12.
[183] 2 Cor 1,12.

Bibliographical Note

- *Dictionary of Paul and His Letters*, InterVarsity Press, Downers Grove (IL) 1993.

Barbaglio G. - Fabris R., *Le lettere di Paolo*, 3 vols., Borla, Roma 1990².

Cipriani S., *Le lettere di S. Paolo*, Cittadella, Assisi 1990⁷.

Hubaut M., *Sur les traces de saint Paul. Guide historique et spirituel*, Desclée de Brouwer, Paris 1995.

Penna A., *Paolo di Tarso. Un cristianesimo possibile*, San Paolo, Cinisello Balsamo 1992.

Pitta A., Paolo. *La vita, le lettere, il suo Vangelo*, San Paolo, Cinisello Balsamo 1997.

Saffrey H. D., *Histoire de l'apôtre Paul*, Les Éditions du Cerf, Paris 1991.

Zedda S., *Prima lettura di San Paolo*, Paideia, Brescia 1973⁵.

Index

Introduction 3

1. Biographical Outline 7

2. The Letters 17

3. Paul's successes and failures as recounted
   in the *Acts of the Apostles* 21

4. Paul's Personality as gleaned
   from the Letters .31

Bibliografical Note 46

Grafiche Grilli srl
Via Manfredonia Km 2,200 - 71100 Foggia (Italy)
Tel. 0881 568040 / 568034 - Fax 0881 755525
www.grafichegrilli.it • e-mail: info@grafichegrilli.it